WORLD IN VIEW
HONG KONG

Nance Lui Fyson

STECK-VAUGHN
LIBRARY

Austin, Texas

Published in the United States in 1991 by Steck-Vaughn Co., Austin, Texas, a subsidiary of National Education Corporation.

This edition originally published 1990 by Heinemann Children's Reference, a division of Heinemann Educational Books Ltd.

Cover: *View from Victoria Peak over Hong Kong Island.*
Title page: *A view of Stanley, a section of Hong Kong Island.*

Designed by Julian Holland Publishing Ltd

Acknowledgments: for Colin

Library of Congress Cataloging-in-Publication Data

Fyson, Nance Lui.
    Hong Kong / Nance Lui Fyson.
      p. cm. — (World in view)
    Summary: Surveys the people, customs, geography, history, economics, food, and contemporary crowded urban lifestyle of Hong Kong.
    ISBN 0-8114-2433-2
    1. Hong Kong—Juvenile literature. [1. Hong Kong.] I. Title.
II. Series.
DS796.H74F97 1990   89-26247
951.25—dc20   CIP
                               AC

Printed and bound in the United States

  2 3 4 5 6 7 8 LB 94 93

Photographic credits:
All photographs by Nance Fyson

Contents

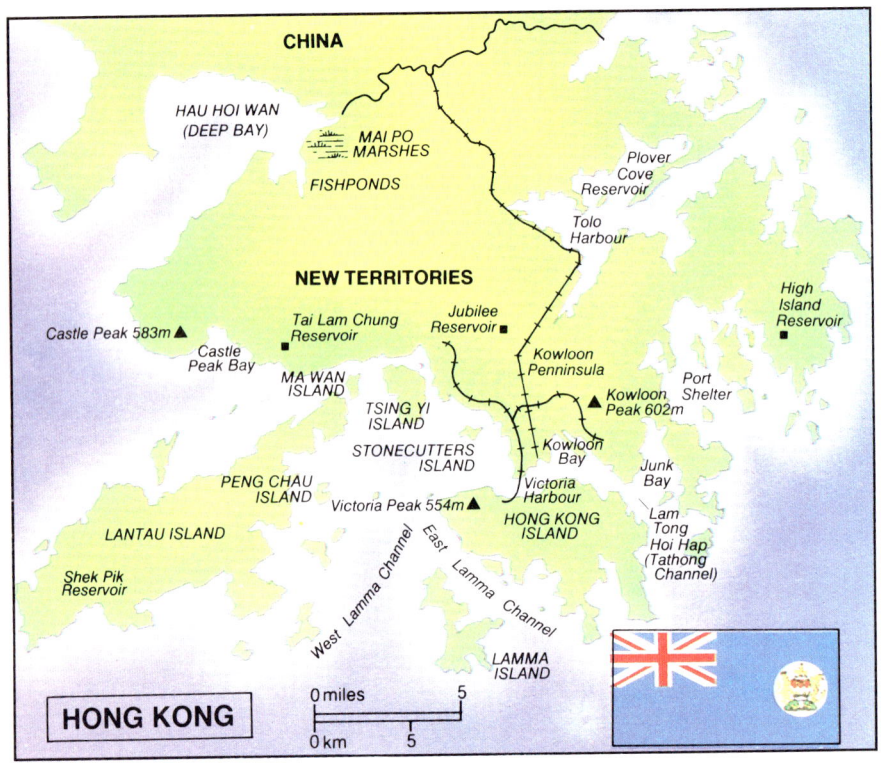

CHINA

HAU HOI WAN
(DEEP BAY)

MAI PO
MARSHES

Plover
Cove
Reservoir

FISHPONDS

Tolo
Harbour

NEW TERRITORIES

High
Island
Reservoir

Castle Peak 583m ▲

Tai Lam Chung
Reservoir

Jubilee
Reservoir ■

Castle
Peak Bay

MA WAN
ISLAND

Kowloon
Penninsula

Port
Shelter

▲ Kowloon
Peak 602m

TSING YI
ISLAND

STONECUTTERS
ISLAND

Kowloon
Bay

Junk
Bay

PENG CHAU
ISLAND

Victoria Peak 554m ▲

Victoria
Harbour

Lam
Tong

LANTAU ISLAND

HONG KONG
ISLAND

Hoi Hap
(Tathong
Channel)

Shek Pik
Reservoir

West Lamma Channel

East Lamma Channel

LAMMA
ISLAND

HONG KONG

0 miles   5

0 km   5

1 Introducing Hong Kong

The bright red street temple is part of the old Chinese religion. Behind the temple is a large bank, part of the new city scene. Hong Kong is full of mixtures of new and old.

Some people think Hong Kong is just one island. In fact, it is a territory that includes 236 islands as well as an area of mainland bordering the southeast coast of China. Hong Kong covers about 386 square miles, and it is a place of many contrasts. There are high-rise buildings and busy city streets, but away from the city centers there are areas of countryside with hardly any people at all. The bustling modern Hong Kong you see in pictures is only part of the story. Over 40 percent of Hong Kong's land is actually green country parks and only nine percent is covered with skyscrapers.

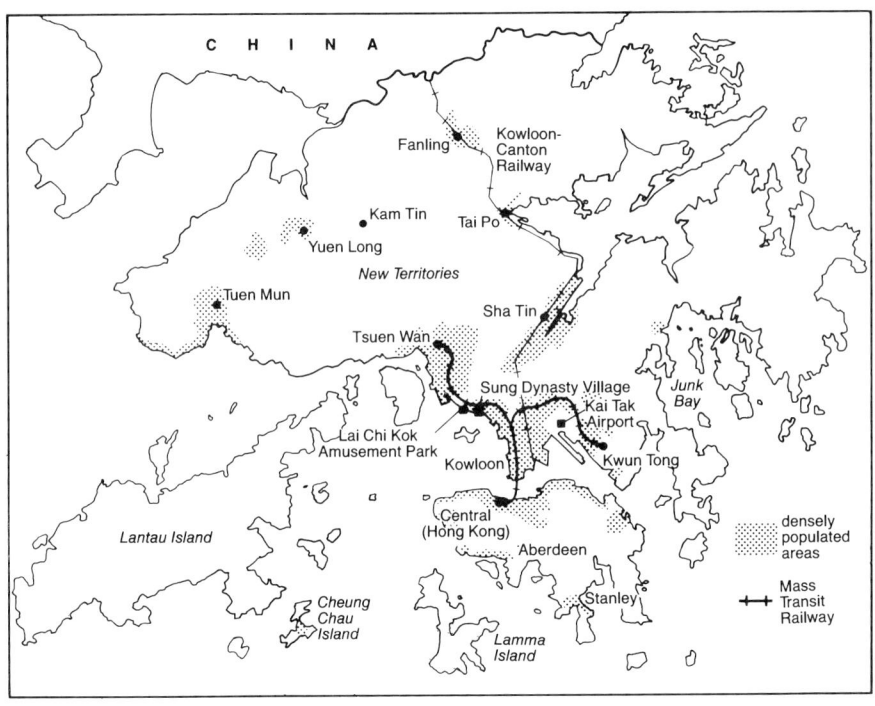

The sharp contrasts of Hong Kong catch the eye. A homeless old person sleeps on the pavement while a big car with a wealthy businessman drives by. A man sits twisting metal puzzles to sell and behind him rises a big glossy bank. Street vendors outside an electronics shop sell lengths of sugarcane to chew. A woman huddles by a steaming cooking pot on her tiny boat, with luxury yachts nearby. A man balances high in the sky tying the bamboo scaffolding used to put up office buildings. Old and new, rich and poor, rough and shiny, the sharp contrasts of Hong Kong are everywhere.

Hong Kong's natural resources
Another contrast is that while many of Hong Kong's islands have few people, other parts of the territory are more crowded than anywhere else in the world. In these parts, land that is flat enough to build houses and offices on is valued highly. "If it doesn't move, build something on it" is a well-known joke in Hong Kong. There is unused land but much of this is just too mountainous to use easily for farming or for building. Hong Kong has, in fact, managed to add over eight square miles of extra land by digging up earth and rocks from the sides of some mountains and placing the rubble on the seabed. The new, reclaimed land is allowed to settle before there is any construction of buildings on it.

Land may be limited, but it is still about the only natural resource Hong Kong has. There is no coal or oil, and the mountains bear only small amounts of a few minerals such as iron, lead, and zinc. Hong Kong even lacks large rivers, lakes, or underground water supplies. Much fresh water is piped, from China. However, the territory is blessed with a deep natural harbor that is one of the best in the world. With such a harbor, trade has become very important, making Hong Kong the busy port it is today. Hong Kong actually takes its name from the Cantonese words *Heung Gong,* which mean "fragrant harbor." (Cantonese is a dialect of Chinese that is widely used in Hong Kong.)

Around the territory

Looking at a map, you can see this important harbor just to the north of an island labeled Hong Kong. It can be confusing, but Hong Kong Island is just one of the islands in the whole territory of Hong Kong. The area of Hong Kong Island called

Stanley, an area on the south coast of Hong Kong Island, is very different from Kowloon, which is seen in the photo opposite.

A large main street in Kowloon. In this busy area of Hong Kong even the overhanging signs crowd each other and hang far out over the street.

Central is the business district, with many big banks. Other areas on the island are just as distinct, and they all have their own special character. Aberdeen is a very old harbor area with many boats on which people live. Stanley, in the far south, was once a fishing village but is now mainly a market and residential area. Causeway Bay on the north coast is the biggest shopping area, with department stores and high-fashion boutiques.

Across the harbor sits another area called Kowloon, which means "nine dragons" in Cantonese. This is much smaller than Hong Kong Island, but has twice the population. Kowloon, like Hong Kong Island, has shops, restaurants, hotels, stores, and many office buildings.

North of Kowloon, an area called the New

Territories borders on China. The New Territories has some farming but is also being built up with new towns to house more of the territory's population. Hong Kong Island, Kowloon, and the New Territories are most important to the economy of Hong Kong and are where most of the people live. However, there are also the outer islands, which are highly valued for their natural beauty.

Lantau Island is nearly twice the area of Hong Kong Island but has a much smaller population. Parts of Lantau have been set aside as nature reserves. Lamma Island has been nicknamed the Stone Age Island because it is still free of cars, motorcycles, high-rise buildings, and factories. These outer islands have green hills and beautiful bays. The narrow lanes of Lamma's main township have stalls selling dried fish, Chinese medicines, and incense. There are also some modern low buildings with banks and shops.

People on Lamma live mainly by fishing, as do people on Cheung Chau, another peaceful island with no vehicles. Boat building is a thriving industry on Cheung Chau. Old-style Chinese boats called junks are made here, as well as new-style fiberglass rowboats and speedboats. Many older buildings in the narrow main streets of Cheung Chau are traditional Chinese shophouses. These have bedrooms and offices upstairs with shops and living rooms below, opening onto the street.

Wildlife

Hong Kong's wide variety of plant and animal life includes the Chinese pangolin or scaly anteater.

This creature is about three feet long, covered in horny scales, and is seen in some rural areas. Monkeys live around the Kowloon reservoirs, and small mammals called shrews can be seen there as well. The Chinese porcupine, with strikingly colored black and white quills, is found in the New Territories and Hong Kong Island.

Wild pigs were once scarce and protected by law, but recently they have increased greatly in number. Farmers now complain that the pigs wander through their fields and damage the crops. The Royal Hong Kong Police Force keeps down the number of wild pigs by killing some.

Larger animals such as the leopard cat, barking deer, and Eastern Chinese otter have been seen in the countryside. As more and more people fill the rural areas, wildlife of this kind is driven away and has no certain home for the future.

Frogs, lizards, and snakes are very common in Hong Kong, but most local snakes are not poisonous. Deaths from snake bites are rare. There are also many local moths and over 200 recorded species of colorful butterflies. One major pest in vegetable gardens is the African giant snail.

The fish and shellfish found in the waters around Hong Kong are mainly tropical. Dolphins can sometimes be seen, and sharks are commonly sighted. There are over 20 different species of shark, and they are mostly found in the waters off the eastern and southeastern coasts.

Conservation
Hong Kong's 21 country parks include woodlands, grass, and scrubs. Many types of

wildlife live in the parks and several laws have been passed to protect animal and plant species in the territory.

Birds are plentiful in Hong Kong, and Mai Po Marshes is a well-known bird sanctuary. Over 250 types of birds have been recorded there, and some of these are quite rare. Another protected area, Yim Tso Ha, has many herons. Birds commonly seen in the woods near old villages include warblers, flycatchers, and robins.

In many rural areas trees are being planted to cover slopes that are almost bare. As people have cut down trees for wood, the hillsides have been left uncovered. If new trees are not planted, Hong Kong's heavy rains wash away the soil.

The Hong Kong Herbarium, with over 35,000 plant species, is more than 100 years old. It is financed by the government and collects preserved plant specimens. Hong Kong also has zoological and botanical gardens, managed by the Urban Council. Stock is bred so that certain types of plants and animals continue to exist.

Climate
Whether people live in the bustling city streets of Hong Kong Island or the quiet peace of Lamma, they share Hong Kong's varied climate. Spring in Hong Kong lasts from March to May with warm days and mild nights. Summer falls between May and September, when daytime temperatures average 86°F and nights are nearly as warm. About 80 percent of the annual rainfall comes in the summer, with June usually being the wettest month. October to December is autumn, when the daytime temperature is about 77°F, and most

days are clear and bright. This is the most popular time for visiting Hong Kong. The winter months of December to February can be quite cool.

Hong Kong's climate is affected by monsoons. These are high winds that come from a certain direction at a particular time of the year. Monsoons are sometimes called trade winds because ancient traders relied on these winds for sailing their ships. The winter monsoon blows in from the north or northeast some time from September to mid-March. The summer monsoon blows in from the south or southwest in the months April to September.

Typhoons

The most serious natural disasters to hit Hong Kong are typhoons. *Tai-fung* is the Chinese word for big wind. About 30 tropical cyclones form in the western North Pacific or in the South or East

In Hong Kong the contrast between rich and poor is often seen. Poor people live on the junks, their only home. In the background are luxury yachts which rich people use for pleasure sailing. These are moored in one of the big shelter areas offering some protection during typhoons.

China Seas each year, and about half reach the high speed of a typhoon. September is the most likely month for typhoons in Hong Kong, but gales may occur from May to November.

One of the territory's worst typhoons was in 1937, when over 1,000 small boats were sunk and 2,500 people were drowned. Typhoon Rose appeared in 1971, hitting the territory with winds of 150 knots and leaving rains of 11.23 inches in a single day.

Hong Kong now has an early warning system to prepare for typhoons. A system of signals from one to ten warns people how close and how powerful the approaching typhoon is. Typhoon Signal 1 goes out when there is a tropical storm within 460 miles of Hong Kong. About once or twice a year warnings with the signal 8 go out on television and radio. This is more serious, and means all offices must shut so that workers can go home before public transportation stops. A signal of 10 means hurricane force winds are expected.

Winds of change
Besides nature's big winds, Hong Kong also has to face the winds of change. In the nineteenth century Hong Kong was described as a "barren and valueless rock." Since then many changes have come to Hong Kong. It has become the world's third most important banking and financial center and one of the world's top 20 trading nations and territories. In 1997, another change is due when Hong Kong ceases to be British and is taken over by the People's Republic of China.

2 Barren Rock to Busy Port

What was Hong Kong like centuries ago? Fishermen had settled on Lamma and Lantau islands and farmers had built walled villages in the New Territories. There were a few communities but not many people lived there and not much had been developed.

The British Foreign Secretary, Lord Palmerston, exaggerated when he described Hong Kong in 1841 as "a barren rock with hardly a house upon it." He thought Britain got a poor deal in becoming the new master of the area. Lord Palmerston thought Hong Kong had no future. Even Great Britain's Queen Victoria didn't think it amounted to much. She said at the time: "Albert (her husband) is so amused at my having got the island of Hong Kong."

The British in China

So why did Hong Kong become a British colony in the 1840s? The answer lies in China, where the British started trading regularly in the seventeenth century. Traders from the East India Company, which was British, arrived in the Chinese city of Canton and had a thriving business buying Chinese tea, silk, and porcelain to take to England. The Chinese Emperor did not like the traders much and thought they were a bad influence on the Chinese people. He kept the *guailo* (foreign devil) traders in a separate area. Foreigners were allowed to stay only for the

15

This is a view of Hong Kong Island from a high point called Victoria Peak. In the distance, across the harbor, is Kowloon. The British who acquired Hong Kong in the 1840s would have been surprised to see how Hong Kong has developed.

trading season and forbidden to learn Chinese.

At that time China accepted only silver bullion for goods. Great Britain wanted to find some other way to pay for all the Chinese goods that were wanted. At the start of the nineteenth century, these traders found an answer. They realized they could buy silks and teas in exchange for the drug opium. The opium was loaded in India and then taken to Canton to be sold. China outlawed the trade in 1799 but the drug had taken its hold on many people. The Chinese Emperor finally assigned a commissioner in 1839 to go to Canton and end the trade in this "foreign mud."

Opium wars

The Chinese commissioner surrounded the British in Canton, cut off their food supplies, and demanded they turn over all the opium they had. The British traders held out for six weeks, but finally gave up 20,000 chests of opium, which were destroyed in public.

Great Britain's Superintendent of Trade in China then attacked Canton in what became known as the first Opium War. The attack resulted in the Convention of Chuen Pi, which allowed the British to use Hong Kong Island. Lord Palmerston had demanded either a commercial treaty putting trade relations on a better footing or a small island where the British could live free from threats. A British Commodore led naval men ashore and claimed Hong Kong Island for Britain in January 1841. Neither China nor Britain were really happy with the terms of Chuen Pi. The loss of a part of China made the Chinese feel shame and anger, and Lord Palmerston thought Hong Kong a poor bargain.

A second Opium War in 1842 ended with the Treaty of Nanking. This officially passed the island of Hong Kong to the British, without any time limit. A third Opium War broke out about the earlier treaties, and a fourth Opium War in 1859 was ended in 1860 by the Convention of Peking. This passed to Great Britain the Kowloon Peninsula, up to the northern limit of what is now Boundary Road. In June 1898, the Second Convention of Peking presented Great Britain with 360 square miles of islands and mainland now known as the New Territories on a 99-year lease from July 1, 1898, to June 30, 1997.

> **Jardine Matheson**
> The nineteenth-century opium traders did much to establish Hong Kong. They dominated Great Britain's foreign relations with China and a company called Jardine Matheson was most important. One of the founders, William Jardine, was a ruthless businessman whom the Chinese regarded as an ''iron-headed rat.'' The Jardine Matheson fortunes were built on opium trading profits.
>
> It was the other partner in the company, James Matheson, who persuaded the British Foreign Office that a permanent base was needed on the China coast. It was also Matheson who chose the site of Hong Kong and who put up the first permanent building. Today, a gun by the Causeway Bay Typhoon Shelter is fired each day at noon. The ritual of the noon gun dates from the mid-nineteenth century and has become a Hong Kong tradition. On New Year's Eve, Jardine's executives also fire the gun at midnight.

The twentieth century

From its opium beginnings, Hong Kong grew fast as a trading center in the twentieth century. Civil war in China during the 1920s and 1930s helped Hong Kong's growth as Chinese businessmen fled with their money to the "safer" area of the British colony. Then came World War II. On December 8, 1941, the Japanese invaded Hong Kong. British military forces were not prepared and on Christmas Day, the British governor surrendered. British power collapsed as quickly in Hong Kong as it did in Singapore. It was August 30, 1945, before the British flag was again raised over Hong Kong. The colony had been ransacked and was in a poor state. During the Korean War, at the start of the 1950s, the colony had to develop other industries besides trade in order to survive. Banking, insurance, and manufacturing started to grow.

The Communists who came to power in China in 1949 chose to leave Hong Kong as it was. The colony was a main source of foreign exchange for

An electronics shop, selling the latest technology. British traders in the nineteenth century never imagined Hong Kong would be such an economic success.

China. At the same time, Hong Kong relied on China's goodwill for its survival. Much of Hong Kong's food and most of its water comes from the People's Republic of China.

1997 time-bomb

Both China and Great Britain had to deal with the problem of what should happen to the New Territories of Hong Kong when the lease expires in 1997. Hong Kong is a reminder to the Chinese of foreigners taking over Chinese land, a symbol of China losing to Japan and Western nations in the nineteenth and early twentieth centuries.

Talks between Great Britain and China about

Schoolgirls in the New Territories wear a uniform that is very much like those worn by many children in Great Britain. No one knows how many British influences will remain after Hong Kong is given back to China in 1997.

Hong Kong began in 1982. After two years of negotiations, an agreement was finally signed in 1984. Great Britain agreed to hand over the whole colony, including Kowloon and Hong Kong Island, to China in 1997. Hong Kong will become a Special Administrative Region of the People's Republic of China. As a special region it will have its own government and legal system and will largely run itself, except for its foreign affairs and defense. The agreement lets Hong Kong keep its present social, economic, and legal system for at least 50 years after 1997. Hong Kong will be allowed to stay a capitalist area while across the border in the People's Republic, the economic system is communist.

The 1984 agreement also guarantees that Hong Kong's people will be allowed to own their property. Hong Kong's residents will also be allowed to travel in and out of the territory. There are to be freedoms like the right to free speech and movement, free choice of job, free religious belief, freedom to hold meetings, and a right for workers to strike. Hong Kong will also stay a free port. This means goods can pass in and out of the port without having any customs duty put on them, so there will still be plenty of trade.

Some people doubt that China's promises about Hong Kong will be kept. No one knows for sure what the leaders will do when the time comes. There is no real guarantee that what is written in the 1984 agreement will occur. Meanwhile, China has been increasing its economic links with Hong Kong. China began a more open economic policy in 1979 and, since 1985, it has been Hong Kong's largest trading partner.

A boutique in Hong Kong, selling the latest fashions. Hong Kong's economy is based on capitalist competition. Those who produce and sell at the best price win.

About 10,000 of Hong Kong's residents a year are so worried about their future in Hong Kong that they choose to leave. Those who can afford to are moving to countries like the United States, Canada, and Australia. British immigration laws have been changed so that only 50,000 of Hong Kong's residents will be allowed to settle in Great Britain as British citizens.

Governing Hong Kong

Part of the 1984 agreement on Hong Kong says that civil servants will keep their jobs after 1997. The 60 or so government departments in the Hong Kong Civil Service employ about 173,000 people. A few thousand of these are foreigners, mainly British, who hold nearly all of the top jobs. This is a reminder that Hong Kong is still very much a British territory. However, the 1984 agreement with China says that foreigners, like the British, cannot be heads of major government departments after 1997. Chinese are gradually being brought in to take over these jobs.

This homeless person sleeping on the street may be among the many people in Hong Kong who don't bother to vote. On the fence behind are campaign posters for an election.

23

The Urban Council looks after recreation areas like this small playground in Kowloon.

At the very top of Hong Kong's government is a governor. There is also an Executive Council (EXCO) which makes government policies. One rung lower is the Legislative Council (LEGCO) which makes laws and controls government money.

The day-to-day running of Hong Kong is the duty of the Urban Council. This council covers matters like street cleaning, garbage collection, running public parks, and issuing licenses to street vendors. The council has 30 members, with 15 appointed and 15 elected by the people. On the next rung down are District Boards. These were set up in 1982 to help Hong Kong residents have some say in their local area. The boards have government officials and elected representatives from the area. These boards have little real power and only about one-sixth of eligible voters even bothers to vote for representatives to the boards. A new Regional Council was set up in 1986 to provide services to expanding new towns in the New Territories.

Hong Kong Island and Mainland Kowloon are home to about half of Hong Kong's people, but the population is growing the fastest in the New Territories. The New Territories is also where some of Hong Kong's local people have lived the longest.

3

People, People, People

With Hong Kong's history, it is not surprising that about 98 percent of the population is Chinese. The only real locals, those who have been on Hong Kong territory for centuries, are the Tankas, Hoklos, and Hakkas.

Boats like those in the picture are home for thousands of people in Hong Kong. Some people are now leaving their boats to live in high-rise apartments like those in the background.

The Tankas are people who fish in local waters. They have traditionally lived on poor, rough boats called junks, and many Tankas rarely come ashore. Junks are moored in protected harbor areas called typhoon shelters. This is a tough life, with little comfort. Smaller boats called sampans are used for traveling around the shelters, and these are paddled by hand or have motors. Women sampan drivers wave an arm around and around to tourists on shore, meaning "do you want to ride around the shelter?"

The Hoklos are also boat people who live on junks, but their boats, their way of talking, and even their hats are slightly different from those of the Tankas. The Tankas fish in deeper waters and have larger boats, while the Hoklo people stay closer to shore. Both groups of boat people have been looked down on by those living on land. The Chinese authorities in Canton used to forbid Tankas and Hoklos to live on shore. In Hong Kong, they were also kept from living on shore until 1911. In recent years, some young people from these communities have chosen to live on land and to work in factories, and the Hong Kong government has encouraged this. Still, the boat communities are busy, thriving places. There are shops, barbers, schools, doctors, and even chickens and temples—all on the boats.

To escape invaders, the Hakka people moved from north to south China hundreds of years ago. They settled in a place now known as the New Territories. Hakka means "guest people" and these people were some of the first refugees in Hong Kong. The Hakkas are farming people, and the older women still wear black pyjamalike

A walled village called Kut Hing Wei in Kam Tin, the New Territories. Inside the outer walls, rows of houses sit between narrow alleylike streets. The Hakka people who live in the village are descended from the Tang clan who built Kut Hing Wei in the 1600s.

clothes with wide-brimmed straw hats fringed in black cloth. Hakka women can be seen selling fruit and vegetables in the market, as well as doing heavy jobs on building sites. Hakka people can also be seen in the six walled villages at Kam Tin in the New Territories. These villages were built in the seventeenth century and are like the traditional walled villages that used to be common in ancient China. There are still guardhouses on the four corners and arrow slits in the walls for fighting off attackers. A small admission fee is charged to tourists who want to go inside the walls. The visitors must also pay to photograph the old women selling paintings and other souvenirs. Babies toddle about in their stylish denim playsuits, in contrast to the traditional clothing of the older generation.

Hakka homes in the Kam Tin village of Kut Hing Wei vary from well-to-do to quite poor. Some houses have ceramic tiles on the walls, and are furnished with televisions, modern sideboards with glass fronts, and cane furniture. A bit farther down narrow alleys are much smaller houses with only cane mats on the floor and old sofas, but also with television sets.

Hakka women work on construction sites in the New Territories. The women are easy to recognize by their wide straw hats which often have a black cloth fringe to help keep out the sun.

A Hakka woman sells vegetables at Luen Wo market. The pyjamalike clothing these women wear is called samfoo.

All the people in a walled village of Kam Tin are likely to be from the same clan, and so share a name. The five great clan names in the New Territories are Tang, Pang, Hau, Liu, and Man.

Immigrants from China
Most of Hong Kong's Chinese population arrived as immigrants during the last 100 years, especially in the last few decades. In 1851, the population of Hong Kong was only about 33,000. In the early part of this century, there were wars and other problems in China that prompted many Chinese to flee to Hong Kong. By the 1930s, the population was over 880,000. At the start of World War II, about 700,000 more people fled from China to Hong Kong. Then the Japanese

invaded in 1941, and by 1945, the population had been reduced by 600,000 as people left or were sent back to China because of food shortages in Hong Kong. When the war ended in 1945, people began coming to Hong Kong again.

The Communists took power in China in 1949, and this prompted another 750,000 people to come to Hong Kong. The population was then about 2.5 million. During the 1950s, 1960s, and 1970s yet more immigrants came across the border from China. Some were legal—but most swam or came in some other illegal way.

"Touchbase"

In the 1960s, the Hong Kong government started a policy that was nicknamed "touchbase." It was something of a game—but serious for the people trying to come to Hong Kong illegally. According to "touchbase," any illegal immigrant who was caught on the border was handed back to the authorities in China. If an immigrant managed to get to a town or city and made contact with friends or relatives, the immigrant was allowed to stay. During the 1960s and 1970s, less than a third of illegal immigrants were being sent back.

By 1980, there were about 3,500 illegal immigrants coming into Hong Kong every day. The police and army could not cope. It was clear that something had to be done, and a tougher policy on immigration was formed. After October 23, 1980, all illegal immigrants from China were returned, regardless of where they were caught. The whole population of Hong Kong was then given three days to register for identity cards. No one could get a job or a home from that day on without an identification card. The news of this spread fast in China. Fewer people tried to enter Hong Kong illegally, but some illegal immigrants still manage to come in today. However, not all immigrants are illegal. About 55,000 immigrants come to Hong Kong legally each year. Most of them have relatives in Hong Kong.

Why people come to Hong Kong

Many people in China have tried to come to Hong Kong because they have heard it is a richer place with more freedoms. Often when people arrive they are disappointed and have problems finding a home. Hong Kong has grown so quickly that not everyone who comes has a good life. By the late 1980s, the population of Hong Kong had grown to nearly six million people.

The insecurity of Hong Kong's Chinese refugee population is part of what has made the territory such an economic success. The Hong Kong Chinese have learned to make the best of whatever circumstances they find. They are adaptable and are used to moving quickly to fill a business need. They work hard and aim to make a success of whatever they do.

Hong Kong's other people

The Chinese are not the only immigrants to have come to Hong Kong. More than 100,000 Vietnamese refugees have also arrived. They are known as boat people because they sailed from Vietnam in tiny boats. Those who have come since 1982 have been put in closed "centers" that they cannot leave until they are resettled in some other country.

People from Vietnam are part of the two percent of Hong Kong's non-Chinese population known to the Chinese as *guailos* (foreigners). The rest of Hong Kong's foreigners are mainly from North America, Europe, and other Asian countries. The British are the largest group of Westerners, but there are sizeable numbers of Americans, Australians, and Canadians as well. Other Asian groups include people from the Philippines, India, Pakistan, Japan, Thailand, Indonesia, and Korea.

Chinese Language

With so many Chinese, it is not surprising that the main language is Cantonese. This is a dialect, or way of speaking, used in southern China. English is also an official language and widely spoken. The main language used in banking, trade, and the law courts is English.

The Chinese language has about eight major dialects. All of these are tonal. This means that the tone of your voice, how you say something, helps decide what the word means. The word written in English as "ma" varies in Cantonese from meaning rope to mother to horse, depending on how you say it.

Sometimes the English used in Hong Kong is a little different from what you would see in North America, Great Britain, or Australia. One shop is called "Very Good Tailor" while another says "Shoes Maker." A department selling eyeglasses in a department store is called "Eye Wears."

Written Chinese has a total of about 50,000 "pictographs," which are characters standing for objects or actions. About 5,000 of these are in

Chinese characters
人 = person
犬 = dog
大 = large
天 = sky

A calligrapher uses a brush to make Chinese characters. Every stroke helps to show the meaning of the word.

common use and you need to know about 1,500 to read a newspaper. Many of the characters you see in Hong Kong are written somewhat differently from the same ones in China.

Every character has a part that gives a clue to how it is pronounced and a part that gives a clue to the meaning. All the characters can be made using about 13 basic strokes. These are always written in a certain order. If one stroke is changed, then the character takes on a different meaning.

Some common words in Cantonese are *Wai!* (for saying hello on the telephone), *Do jeh* (thank you, for a gift), *Hou* for yes, and *Mhou* for no. All of these can be written as pictographs as well. Another very common word in Hong Kong is *joss* which means luck.

4 Beware of Sleeping Dragons

Trying for good luck is important to the Chinese. If you want "joss" you must please the gods and drive away bad spirits. The Chinese think that many dragons lie sleeping in the earth, and that they must be kept happy to keep good fortune on your side. Religion and superstition are closely linked. Incense in the form of joss sticks is burned at temples and home shrines. Often the sticks are held upright by being stuck into oranges or even halves of apples.

Joss sticks are made from bamboo that is split thinly. The sticks are put into a mixture of incense powder, sawdust, and a scented substance such as rose powder. Coated sticks are then dried.

Lucky numbers are also important. Rich people in Hong Kong pay thousands of dollars to have a car license plate with good numbers. The lucky numbers are two (meaning easy), three (living or giving birth), six (a long life), eight (prosperity), and nine (eternity). Combinations of numbers can be very lucky as well. A number like 168 is popular as it means lifelong prosperity.

Just as some numbers are lucky, some numbers are thought to be especially unlucky. In the Cantonese language, the word for four is very like the word for death. Therefore, anything with the number four is to be avoided. On Hong Kong Island there is a power station with five chimney stacks, but only four are used. The fifth is just pretend, to avoid having four.

Joss sticks are lit outside the Wong Tai Sin temple in Kowloon. These sticks are burned to bring good luck.

Fung-shui

Chinese don't leave their luck to chance. Even buildings must be put up in the best place and must face the right way to bring the best luck. *Fung-shui* (wind-water) is the art of judging the best way of arranging the environment. Before a high-rise apartment or a shiny modern office building is put up, experts on jung-shui are asked for their advice. They survey the site, checking both the currents that swirl around the surface of

Jade

The semiprecious stone jade, in varying shades of green and other colors, is thought by the Chinese to be lucky and also to bring good health. Jade can be carved into very ornate designs. At an outdoor Jade Market in Kowloon there are stalls with bracelets, earrings, rings, and carvings, as well as uncut stones. Traders bid for uncut jade, using secret signs with their hands hidden behind newspapers as they bargain.

Strangely enough, the word jade comes from a Portuguese word meaning kidneys. The first jade was brought back to Europe by early Portuguese and Spanish explorers. They had been told it was a stone that could ward off kidney diseases.

Many people in Hong Kong, even little children, now wear some piece of jade as a lucky charm. In ancient times, well-to-do Chinese were even buried in suits of jade. Jade green is also a popular color for refrigerators and washing machines.

Jade in many shades of green and other colors is sold in the outdoor Kowloon Jade Market. Some pieces are cheap while others are very expensive. The larger jade circles are arm bangles and the small circles are rings. Many Chinese wear jade to bring them luck.

the earth and the dragons sleeping below the ground. Neither should be disturbed by humans. The fung-shui experts warn against the anger of a sleeping dragon who wakes to find a high-rise apartment building on his tail.

Fung-shui experts are even contacted before telephone poles are put up or highways are laid. The underground train system (MTR) in Hong Kong was built only after priests paid respect to the spirits of the earth whose home was about to be disturbed.

Outside the glossy modern Hong Kong and Shanghai Bank in Hong Kong there are two bronze lions. These are not set squarely to each other and the reasons for this is fung-shui. According to fung-shui, objects are positioned so as to bring good fortune. Another big modern building in Hong Kong is the Connaught Center on the waterfront. This is supposed to have bad fung-shui and many Chinese do not want to go in the building, let alone work there.

According to fung-shui, it is also unlucky to allow good winds that enter a building to blow straight out the other side. For this reason, doors and windows are not put opposite in a room.

Chinese religion

The belief that there are living spirits in trees, rocks, and the ground is called animism. According to traditional Chinese religion, a priest should be called in even before a tree is chopped down, because it might have a spirit living in it. Traditionally, villagers planted groves of trees around the settlement to house good spirits who prevent sickness.

The Hong Kong and Shanghai Bank building in the Central part of Hong Kong Island is the most expensive building in the world. Fung-shui experts helped decide how it should be built.

Chinese religion is also a mixture of the three main philosophies, Taoism, Confucianism, and Buddhism. There are Christians, Jews, Moslems, Sikhs, and Hindus in Hong Kong as well, but most people follow Chinese religion.

Taoism apparently was founded by Lao-tzu who lived many years ago, about 604 B.C. Tao is a way of life in which people try to live in harmony with the universe. Taoism teaches that life's mysteries can be known only by leading a peaceful life and by thinking deeply and clearly.

Confucius, who founded Confucianism, was born into a poor family around 551 B.C. He held some government jobs and then looked for a way that would help people live together peacefully. He taught that if a person has the right attitude, then he will have respect for himself, and a sense of the dignity of human life. To Confucius, the ideal person was fearless, even tempered, and nonviolent.

According to Confucian ideas, what a person does always affects others. A person must make sure that his actions do not make difficulties for others. Confucianists also think the family is the most important unit in society. Children must have respect for their parents. This respect and duty flows toward one's elders and superiors, from young to old and employee to boss.

The idea of face, or dignity, is also important to Confucian thought. Letting down the family or group by falling short of what they expect is a source of great shame for the Chinese.

Taoism and Confucianism started in China, but Buddhism began in India. The founder lived about the sixth century B.C. and was called Siddhartha Guatama. He was a prince who decided to search for enlightenment, or an understanding of life, and he founded an order of monks. Siddhartha thought that desire is the cause of unhappiness. He said that happiness can only be reached if desires are overcome. Buddhism developed in China during the third to sixth centuries A.D.

Polytheism

The founders of Taoism, Confucianism, and Buddhism are all worshiped as gods by the Chinese. Many other gods are worshiped as well. Some of these are people in history who did heroic deeds. Worshiping many gods is called polytheism (poly means many).

One of the most popular goddesses in Hong Kong is Tin Hau, Queen of the Sea and Protector of Seafarers. She was a real person who lived in the eleventh century. Even as a child she was good at forecasting weather, which made her a favorite with fishermen. There is now even a Festival of Tin Hau on the 23d day of the third month each year. The special Tin Hau Temple comes alive during the festival, with gaily decorated boats passing by. Fishermen pray for clear skies and lots of fish.

Temples

The Tin Hau temple is just one of many in Hong Kong. Chinese temples are usually green or yellow and are decorated with figures of gods and lucky symbols like fish. Stone lions often guard the entrances. Inside one of these temples sits a small courtyard with a large bowl where incense and paper offerings are burned. Beyond that comes a hall with an altar table with offerings of fruit and drink. The altar has images framed by red brocade embroidered with gold. Temple roofs are steeply curved so that any evil spirit that tries to sit on top of the temple will slide down and have to fly away.

One of the most famous temples in Hong Kong is Wong Tai Sin, which is surrounded by public

An altar table in a Chinese temple.

housing in Kowloon. The temple is named for a shepherd boy who, at the age of fifteen, was taught by a god to cure illness using a special drug. Wong Tai Sin went on to be a famous healer and he is worshiped today by people worried about health, family, or business problems.

Fortune telling
Nearly everyone who visits Wong Tai Sin temple wants his or her fortune told. This is done by

Children at Wong Tai Sin temple shake a chim until a numbered stick falls out. The children will take their sticks to a fortune-teller.

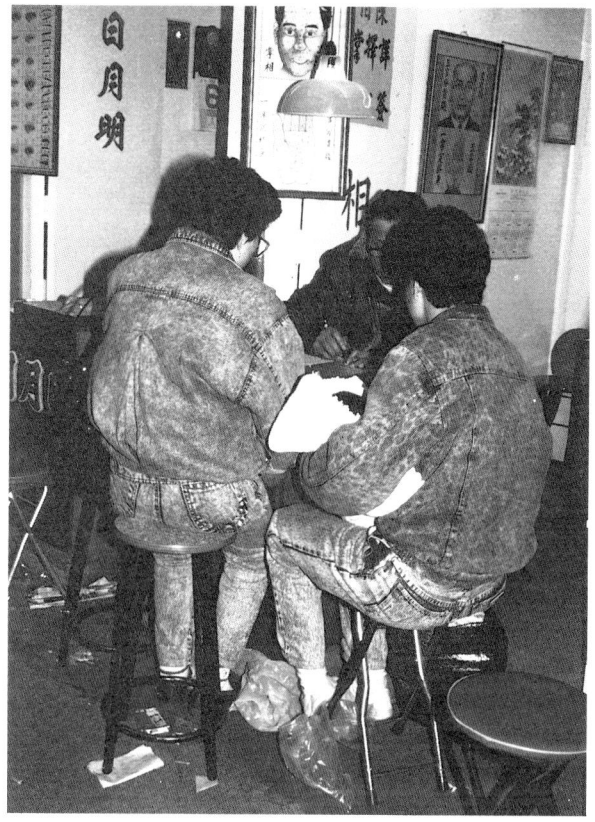

A young couple see a fortune-teller at Wong Tai Sin temple. Many Chinese rely on fortune-tellers for advice about problems and to tell them what the future will bring.

using a bamboo container, a *chim*, which holds numbered sticks. Joss sticks are lit and the worshiper kneels down in front of the main altar. He or she makes a wish and shakes the container gently until a stick falls out. The stick is exchanged for a piece of paper bearing the same number. The fortune written on the paper is interpreted by a soothsayer. Temple keepers charge for interpreting fortune papers. Another way to get advice is by tossing *sing pui*. These are

43

two pieces of wood with irregular sides that show yes or no in answer to a question.

Temples often also have shelves housing the *tai sue*, the gods in charge of each year of the Chinese calendar. Worshipers make offerings to the god of the year in which they were born.

Animal Year Charts show the 12 animal signs of the rat, ox, tiger, rabbit, dragon, snake, horse, sheep, monkey, rooster, dog, and boar. Each of these appears once every 12 years, in a cycle. Following Chinese tradition, people born under different signs show different characteristics. For example, those born in the year of the Tiger (. . . 1950, 1962, 1974 . . .) will be aggressive. Those people born in the year of the Sheep (. . . 1955, 1967, 1979 . . .) will be gentle and mild.

A person's animal sign is not the only way to tell his or her fate. The hour and day of birth are important, as is a person's *Ying* and *Yang*. Yin represents the earth and female, while Yang stands for the sky and male. Everyone needs balance and harmony between their Yin and Yang.

It is said that the animal year chart started when Buddha ordered all the beasts of the earth to gather before him. Only 12 animals came and they were rewarded by having their names given to a year. The Buddha also decided to name each year in the order in which the animals gathered. The rat was first to appear.

Two calendars

People in Hong Kong live both by the calendar that is used in North America and Europe and by the Chinese lunar calendar. The word lunar means that the calendar is based on the changes in the moon. Most festivals are set by the lunar calendar and so the dates vary from year to year. The lunar calendar has 12 months per year, just like the Western calendar. The difference is that each lunar month lasts exactly 30 days.

Chinese New Year

The Chinese celebrate when one animal year changes to another. Chinese New Year falls around the end of January or the beginning of February, depending, of course, on the lunar calendar. In the past the celebrations went on for a week to ten days. Now three days suffice.

New Year is a family holiday when houses are cleaned, debts are paid, and arguments are made up. Thousands of people in Hong Kong go to China to see relatives. Pictures of gods are pasted up around the front doors of houses to scare off evil spirits. Messages of welcome are written on red paper to encourage good spirits. Everyone gets double wages, and around this time even a haircut is likely to cost twice as much.

Lucky money, *lai-si*, is given in red envelopes as tips to tradespeople. Children are also given little red lai-si packets of money. The traditional greeting at this time is *Kung hey fat choi*, meaning good wishes, good fortune.

It is believed that the Kitchen God visits households to report on how a family has behaved during the year. Chinese families prepare a sticky sweet *tang kwa* and put this on the god's lips so that only sweet words will be said. On the night before New Year's Day, the Chinese buy lucky peach blossoms and kumquat trees at huge flower fairs.

At the end of Chinese New Year which is between the middle and the end of February, lanterns with traditional designs are lit in homes, restaurants, and temples. This is called *Yuen Siu*, or the Lantern Festival.

Other festivals

Ching Ming is a family festival usually held in April. This is a time for visiting and taking care of graves, and leaving food and wine for the spirits. Incense and paper money are burned at the graveside for the dead.

Funerals are lavish occasions in China. Centuries ago the Chinese buried horses, carriages, and even wives and servants to keep the dead happy. Today, it is common to burn paper models of objects like cars and televisions as well as bundles of paper money so the dead person is comfortable in the next life. Graves are usually placed on the side of a hill so that the deceased has a good view. The Chinese think it is important to please the dead so they will grant favors to the living.

Bodies are first buried in temporary graves while relatives ask fung-shui experts to find the right burial site. After seven years, the bones are dug up and cleaned and put in an urn that the family keeps. It may be many years before the bones are buried in their final place. Today, however, cremation is becoming more common since land for burial is so scarce.

Another celebration is the Bun Festival of *Tai Chiu*. This is held each May on Cheung Chau

Island. The festival began many years ago to please the evil spirits who caused a bad storm and an epidemic of illness. On the first day of the celebrations, three 66-foot towers of buns are mounted on bamboo scaffolding near the waterfront. On the third day there is a procession with floats.

In late May, the birthday of Lord Buddha is celebrated. Statues of the Buddha are taken from temples and are bathed in scented water. People drink the water afterward, believing it is good for curing illness.

The Dragon Boat Festival takes place in June. Long, narrow boats with dragon heads at one end and dragon tails at the other are rowed with much noise and celebration. The event marks a sad story. A poet many centuries ago threw himself in the river to protest against a bad government. People living by the river threw dumplings in the water to keep the hungry fish away from him. People today eat rice dumplings at the time of the festival in memory of the poet.

Toward the end of August the Festival of the Hungry Ghosts, *Yen Lo*, is celebrated in a way that is similar to Halloween. The Chinese believe that the keeper of the underworld allows ghosts out of hell to roam the earth for 24 hours. To please the spirits, food is offered and images of the gods of hell are burned at the end of the festival.

In September or October the Mid-Autumn Festival is held, and it is very popular with children. As the full moon rises, children carry paper lanterns to open places to admire the moon. They eat moon cakes made of ground sesame seeds and dates.

The dragon dance has groups of performers with the "body" of a fierce dragon. This is popular at festivals and official ceremonies.

Entertainment

Festivals are generally lively occasions and there is often entertainment as well. Lion dances are performed by young men in colorful costumes. There are usually performances of Chinese Opera, which is a mixture of singing, speaking, mime, acrobatics, and dancing that goes on for five or six hours.

Puppet shows are popular as well. Different kinds of puppets are used. Rod puppets are fixed to a long pole and moved by short sticks. String puppets are moved by strings. Shadow puppets are made from leather and are held up against a silk screen to cast shadows.

Weddings

Weddings are another excuse for celebrating. The color red is lucky, so the bride's dress is red and the groom wears a red sash. In the villages there are still some arranged marriages, and parents ask a matchmaker to find a partner for their son or daughter. A fortune teller then checks the times of the birthdays to see if the match is a good one. Young people in city areas mostly find their own partners, but it is usual to ask the consent of parents. Special foods are served at weddings since, for the Chinese, food and the art of cooking are very important indeed.

5 "Good Food Is First Happiness"

With so many Chinese people, the food in Hong Kong is mainly Chinese. Foods from other parts of the world, including fast-food hamburgers, are available, but the delight of Hong Kong is the wide range of Chinese dishes. Even toppings on pizza have an oriental style.

Chinese cooking is one of the finest cuisines in the world. Chinese people take great care over producing and eating good food. Flavor, color, and texture are important. A good Chinese meal has to have the right mix of sweet and sour, crunchy and tender. The Chinese like to use fresh food and many people in Hong Kong shop more than once a day. "Good food is first happiness," said Confucius in the fifth century B.C..

Shortages of food and even famines have made the Chinese very resourceful. In times of hunger, the Chinese have learned to make the most of foods that some other people wouldn't eat. Anything that "keeps its back to heaven" is considered fit to consume. Snakes, eels, sharks, lizards, sparrows, and pigeons are some of the various meats used in cooking. "If it moves eat it" is an old Chinese saying.

The Chinese also use parts of animals that might seem unusual, making delicious meals out of such things as pig's brains and chicken blood or bear paws. The paws need to be cooked for 16 hours to make them tender. Even fish eyes and lips are a delicacy. Bird's nest soup is made from

Chopsticks are used for eating instead of a knife and fork. For this meal the metal bowl on the right sits over a lit burner and is full of boiling water. Raw foods like the meat on the plate at the left are dipped in the water to cook quickly.

the dried lining of a sea swallow's nest. No part of an animal is wasted. Food is an important part of life, and the frequent greeting of one friend to another in Hong Kong is *"Nei sik jo fan mai a?"* "Have you had your rice yet?"

The Chinese people in Hong Kong come from many parts of China, but most are from the south where rice is the main food.

Regional cooking

The Cantonese style of cooking, from the south of China, is the most common in Hong Kong. Foods are steamed or quickly stir-fried in a low curved cooking dish called a *wok*. China and Hong Kong are short of fuel for cooking so woks are a good way of cooking quickly and saving energy. As in

51

much of China, chicken and pork are the most popular meats. Steamed white rice is usually served with a Cantonese meal, and the Chinese eat with chopsticks instead of knives and forks.

Popular Cantonese food includes the local fish *garoupa*, which is steamed with ginger, spring onions, soy sauce, and a touch of garlic. Another favorite is sweet and sour prawns (fresh prawns in a sauce of sugar, vinegar, soy sauce and ketchup, colored with green and red peppers). There is also lemon chicken, with chunks of tender chicken cooked in a creamy sauce of corn starch, lemon juice, and chicken broth. Crabmeat and corn soup is a thick broth full of crab and kernels of corn. The Chinese usually have soup toward the end of a meal, except for shark's fin soup, which is special and is served as a middle course. It may have mushrooms, chicken, and bacon or ham in it as well as shark's fin.

While Hong Kong Chinese food is much the same as that eaten in China, there are some differences. For example, dog is a delicacy in China, but eating dog is not allowed officially in Hong Kong.

Beijing cooking
Beijing is the northern Chinese style of cooking, but it is also found in Hong Kong. Wheat, not rice, is the main food in the north of China so this style of cooking features noodles and dumplings, as well as bread. One favorite dish is crispy duck, which is honey-coated before roasting. Chunks of duck plus spring onions and sweet plum sauce are put on pancakes and then rolled up. Another favorite Beijing-style dish is hot and sour soup

Dried prawns of varying quality are sold at different prices. The abacus (below right) is still used by many shopkeepers for counting.

made of shredded pork, bamboo shoots, bean curd, spring onions, and mushrooms.

Mongolian hot-pot is cooked on a small charcoal stove placed in the center of the table. Very thin slices of meat and fish are served raw. You cook the meal yourself by dipping the slices into boiling water, using small wire baskets. A spicy sauce is then used for a dip.

53

Shanghai and Sichuan (Szechuan) cooking

Shanghai cooking is from the east of China and has heavier, richer flavors. One popular dish is Beggar's Chicken. The chicken is cooked in a clay pack which is then cracked open with a hammer at the table. Besides chicken, there are usually mushrooms, pickled cabbage, shredded pork, bamboo shoots, and wine in the stuffing.

Sichuan cooking is western Chinese cooking, and it is the spiciest. Smoked duck, marinated in rice wine with ginger and spices, is one dish. Deep-fried beef with carrots, celery, and peppers is another.

Drinks and baked goods

Tea, without milk and sugar, is the popular drink. The favorite is jasmine-scented green tea or black tea. People in Hong Kong also drink beer, rice wine, and brandy. Supermarkets and shops stock colorful cartons of drinks. On display are mango juice, lime juice, herb tea, coconut-flavored soy milk, melon-flavored soy milk, and even sugarcane juice.

Bakeries sell delicious buns and breads, sometimes with fillings. There is also red bean bun (with the beans baked in), and chicken bread and sausage bread (with the chicken and sausage mixed into the dough before the bread is baked).

Restaurants

Eating out is very common in Hong Kong, and there are more restaurants there than almost anywhere else on earth. Part of the reason is that many homes are a lot of apartments with people living closely together. People often go out to eat

Breakfast and *dim sum*
Early in the morning, all over Hong Kong, the Chinese breakfast on noodles or *congee*. Congee is a rice porridge with an added foodstuff such as salted fish. Otherwise, breakfast might be noodle soup with chunks of vegetables and pork.

Lunch in Hong Kong is often tea and *dim sum*. These are delicious snacks eaten from morning to mid-afternoon, often in a dim sum restaurant. There are about 2,000 different types of dim sum, but restaurants may each offer only a few dozen kinds. Servers wander from table to table with their carts. Steaming bamboo baskets hold dishes like steamed dumpling stuffed with minced pork, or steamed rice flour dumplings filled with assorted meat. Another offering might be deep-fried spring rolls filled with shredded pork, chicken, mushrooms, bamboo shoots, and bean sprouts. Dessert might be a crisp and sticky sweet cake topped with almonds. In a dim sum restaurant you order food from carts and then, at the end of the meal, a waiter counts the number of empty dishes and gives you a bill.

Dim sum means literally "little heart" or "touching the heart." These delicious snacks are eaten from morning to mid-afternoon.

55

Caged birds are a much-loved pet and are taken out for "walks." In Hong Kong men may go out for a dim sum and tea break, some taking their pet birds. Some restaurants have poles strung across so these birds can be hung up while the men enjoy dim sum and a good chat.

and to entertain. Besides indoor restaurants, there are simple outdoor restaurants where the cooking and eating is in alleys and back streets.

There are no napkins on tables in most Hong Kong restaurants but you are served a small, warm, damp towel to wash with after, and sometimes also before, a meal.

Floating restaurants are also part of Hong Kong life. For example, in Causeway Bay you can be rowed out to a whole fleet of simple restaurants on boats. These have tables and chairs and the cooking is done on the boats as well.

One restaurant in Kowloon has 308 dishes on the menu. These range from no. 96, braised chicken and bamboo shoots with bean paste, to no. 166, braised eggplant in garlic chili sauce. (Braising is a cross between baking and steaming.) There are braised pig's intestines, pig's tendon with shrimp eggs, and white eels with brown sauce. The waiter brings hot herb tea in glasses to the table as customers decide what to order. The kitchens in large restaurants often have racks of wooden clothespins with table numbers on them. These are pinned to dishes so the right food gets to the right table. Restaurants sometimes have a small religious alcove lit by red bulbs, with joss sticks burning inside.

Food production
Much of Hong Kong's food comes from outside the territory. Only about nine percent of the total land area is suitable for growing crops, with only two percent of the work force in farming and fishing.

Local farmers do manage to produce quite a lot

A seller in a New Territories fish market weighs fish on a hand-held ching scale. This way of measuring is over 2,000 years old.

of food, however. This includes about 30 percent of Hong Kong's fresh vegetables, over half the chickens and ducks, about 20 percent of pigs, 14 percent of freshwater fish, and 90 percent of marine fish eaten. People in Hong Kong prefer fresh to chilled or frozen food, so local produce helps fill that demand. About 16 percent of what

Hong Kong imports from China is food.

China now supplies a lot of rice to the territory. In 1954, Hong Kong used nearly 2,500 acres of land to grow rice. By 1985, less than 25 acres of land were being used. The rice is grown in terraced paddy fields. These are water-logged and the water comes from a very old network of irrigation. Instead of growing rice, farmers now produce vegetables, which earn them more money. Main vegetable crops include cabbages, lettuce, Chinese kale, radishes, and spring onions, which are grown throughout the year. In summer, spinach, string beans, cucumbers, and Chinese gourds are grown. A wide range of vegetables including tomatoes, sweet pepper, celery, cauliflower, and carrots are grown in winter.

Hong Kong also grows fruit such as lychees, tangerines, lemons, bananas, and guavas. The amount of orchard land has been increasing since the 1950s. Other crops such as sugarcane or starchy root crops like sweet potatoes, taro, and yams are grown on a small scale. There is not much grazing land, so pigs and poultry are the main animals reared for food.

Fishing industry
Catching marine fish is an important industry for Hong Kong, with over 150 species of fish found in nearby waters. Moreover, in the New Territories, there is pond fish farming, with various species of carp grown in artificial ponds. However, as the new towns grow, less land is used for fish farming. Government advisers are developing new methods to increase production.

6   Caring for People

Advisers to farmers and fishermen are just some of the people paid by the government. In Hong Kong, one in every four dollars is spent by the government. In the 1950s, this was much lower, only about one dollar in every ten. Hong Kong is still far behind most European countries. However, social welfare spending in Hong Kong is expanding.

A public assistance program aims to increase the income of needy families to a certain level. There are also programs to help the elderly, especially with housing. Traditionally, elderly Chinese people always lived with their families and were cared for by them. In modern city life, the traditional family life is declining. The government realizes a need for more senior citizen housing and self-care hostels for some of the elderly. Another program called Opportunity for Youth encourages young people to find areas of need in their community and to suggest projects that will help others.

Education

The government spends a great deal of money on young people and their education. Since 1971, parents have not had to pay to send their children to primary schools run by the government. For those who can afford it, there are also private fee-paying schools, and private kindergartens for children aged three to five.

After six years of primary school, children move on to junior secondary school. They take a

This class in Aberdeen on Hong Kong Island is remedial, for slow learners. The teacher uses a microphone so that everyone can hear clearly. Most classes in the school have about 40 pupils but this class is special with only 20.

test to see what type of school they should attend. There are four main types of secondary schools. Some schools are for those planning to go to a university, while others are for those who will eventually learn a technical or commercial skill.

Anglo-Chinese grammar schools are the most academic secondary schools. The course lasts five years, and covers a range of subjects leading to the Hong Kong Certificate of Education Examination (HKCEE). The teaching is mainly in English. Students leaving may well go on to one of Hong Kong's two universities. The University of Hong Kong opened in 1911 and uses English as its main language. The Chinese University in the New Territories is much newer, and most classes are taught in Chinese.

Chinese middle schools also have courses leading to the HKCEE but teaching is mainly in Chinese, with English as a second language. Technical schools teach mainly technical and commercial subjects and students may go on to technical institutions or polytechnics afterward. Prevocational schools provide a general education and introduction to technical skills. Many students leave to enter craft apprenticeship programs.

Adult education offers course and recreational activities for adults and young people no longer in formal education. Topics cover a variety of subjects, from knitting to microcomputers. Educational television for schools covers the Chinese language, the English language, math, social studies, science, and some health education as well.

Health problems

As part of health education, pupils in secondary schools are taught about the dangers of taking drugs. This is a major problem in Hong Kong, where there are nearly 50,000 heroin addicts. The government is trying to stop heroin from entering the country, and is also trying to show people the way that drugs can harm their health.

The main causes of death in Hong Kong today are various types of cancer, heart disease, and diseases of circulation and the blood. These are similar to the main causes of death in richer Western nations such as the United States and Great Britain. In Hong Kong, people can, on average, expect a long life—averages of 74 years for men and 80 years for women.

One difference between Hong Kong and richer nations is that some diseases like tuberculosis are still a major problem in Hong Kong. There are also tropical infections like malaria, which can be spread when a certain type of mosquito bites a person. The government displays posters and pamphlets reminding the public not to leave stagnant pools of water where the insects can breed. Virus hepatitis A and hepatitis B are health hazards in Hong Kong as well. Since 1981, AIDS (Acquired Immune Deficiency Syndrome) has affected thousands of people.

Health care

Outpatient clinics in Hong Kong charge patients only a small fee. The cost of health care is partly paid for by the government. If the patient has no money and this is recorded by a social worker, then the person may not be charged a fee at all.

Mobile clinics and even floating clinics take medical services to outlying islands and remote areas. There is also a "flying doctor" service, with aircraft used to take doctors to patients. Family Health services offer various services including family planning (birth control). People are being encouraged to limit the size of their families.

In addition to government and government-assisted hospitals, there are also private hospitals for people who want to pay for special care.

Traditional medicine

The Chinese also believe in using herbs, roots, and other plant parts as medicines. Shops selling traditional Chinese medicine have bags and counters stocked with remedies that have been

A woman in a medicine shop shows birds' nests which are used to help clear colds and sore throats. The lining of a nest is steamed in a healthy soup.

used for thousands of years. Mushrooms are used to treat cancer. Ginger is widely used for stomach problems and other ailments.

Bright neon lights on the streets of Kowloon advertise acupuncture, which is also part of traditional medicine. This way of treating diseases began in China about 4000 B.C. The ancient acupuncturist used a sharp stone to press various parts of the body in order to cure sick

63

Brightly lit shops sell herbs, roots, and other raw plant materials used in traditional medicine. Sometimes Chinese doctors send people to the shops to buy specific materials. People learn from an early age what is good for various ailments. Sometimes customers just ask the sales people what should be bought and how some mixtures should be made.

people. The stone was later replaced by needles made of bone or bamboo. When metals were discovered, needles of copper, iron, and silver came into use.

Acupuncturists today put fine stainless steel needles into the skin. From 1 to 30 needles are used, depending on the complaint. The points at which the needles are inserted are carefully located and are called acupuncture points. There are in fact over 600 of these points on the body, though only about 200–300 are used regularly.

Since 1959, acupuncture has been used successfully as a pain-killing anaesthetic during operations. People can stay conscious during surgery and yet feel no pain.

Acupuncture is based on the ancient Chinese philosophy that two balancing principles, *Yang* and *Yin*, run the universe. When these forces are out of balance in the human body, illness occurs. The energy of life, *Chi'i*, is thought to flow along paths in the body. Acupuncturists insert needles at chosen points along these paths. This is to correct the flow of energy and thus cure disease.

Housing problems

Poor health may be due to an imbalance of Yin and Yang, but overcrowded and poor housing do not help. About half of the people in Hong Kong live in housing that is not adequate. With so many refugees, the population has grown so fast that housing is a big problem.

The pressure can be noticed in many ways. Folding tables are featured in home furniture departments as a good way of saving space. A secondhand furniture shop sells a bunk bed, with a double bed for parents on the bottom and a single bed above for a child. It is quite common to find families of five or more living in one room.

Children are often encouraged not to show feelings. This makes it easier for people to live closely together without arguing. Getting along with others is essential with so little space.

There are only a few hundred single houses on Hong Kong Island. Land is much too costly to build many one- or two-story buildings. Anyone owning a house on the island is certain to be a millionaire. Most people live in high-rise apartment buildings.

For immigrants who have just arrived, housing is whatever makeshift cover they can manage. This might be a large wooden crate by the side of the road. With rough windows and doors cut out, this crate may have to be a temporary home for a family.

Squatting

Settling with no legal right is called "squatting," and it is very common in Hong Kong. When refugees poured into the territory just after World War II, they had no choice but to squat. The government tried to ignore the problem.

In 1953, a fire swept through a squatter camp in Kowloon and 50,000 people became homeless. This pushed the government into action. The public works department built some two-story apartment buildings as emergency housing. During the next year, a resettlement department was set up to rehouse people.

By the mid-1980s, over 120,000 families were squatting. Some squatter areas have now become legal, and if huts have numbers on them they are allowed to stay. For illegal squatters, life is very insecure. The housing department has a squatter control division that checks daily for illegal huts. Teams of workmen with bulldozers and crowbars pull down any huts that are not legal. About 250 huts are taken down each week by the unit. Many of these illegal huts are built by organized crime in Hong Kong called the *Triads*. (Triads are also involved in gambling, street crime, and other activities where there is illegal money to be made.) People pay members of the Triads a sum of money and for this they get a hut, basic sanitation, a hook-up to a power line, and water.

Fire is still a common problem for squatters. Kerosene stoves are used for cooking, and fires break out easily. After a fire, squatters register with a government agency and have to prove they are real victims. If their case is thought to be real, some help is given. Usually this is only a rolled-up mat, a couple of blankets, and some utensils for cooking.

Temporary Housing Areas

Slightly better than squatter areas are the Temporary Housing Areas (THAs). There are over 40 of these around Hong Kong, housing about 90,000 people. The government supplies a basic wooden shed and residents are given wood, corrugated iron, and some tools. Water supplies, sanitation, and power are provided, but life is not very comfortable in the camps. Families pay a small amount of money to the government to live in the THAs.

Rough housing like this, made from scraps of wood and corrugated iron, is home for thousands of people in Hong Kong.

Housing near the China border is traditional, with covered porches and alleyways between homes. The women use the space for a game of mahjong.

Public housing

Ever since the early 1950s, the government has become more and more involved with public housing. By 1982 the Hong Kong Housing Authority controlled nearly half a million apartments and was the largest landlord in the world. By 1987, over 48 percent of Hong Kong's people were living in public housing.

Beside rented apartments, some housing is bought at reduced prices from the government. The Home Ownership Scheme (HOS) and Private Sector Participation Scheme (PSPS) allow lower-middle income families the chance to buy their own apartments at lower prices.

New towns

In 1972, a major new housing program was started. The aim was to build new towns in the New Territories to provide more housing. Tsuen Wan, Tuen Mun, and Sha Tin were the first generation of new towns. Building in Sha Tin began in 1973 and 30 villages are being absorbed by the city as it grows. The plan is for a mixture of housing, with over half publicly owned.

High-rise apartments in new towns are changing the landscape of the New Territories in a dramatic way.

The New Towns Program has meant much more than just building public housing. Before building, land has had to be formed, much of it by filling in the seabed with material from the hillsides. This has been necessary because so much of Hong Kong's land area is rugged hillside not suitable for development.

By 1987, over 200,000 public housing apartments and over 130,000 private housing units had been built. The population of all the new towns has risen to two million, over a third of Hong Kong's total population. The first new towns are growing and developments continue in later new towns such as Tai Po, Fanling, Yuen Long, and Junk Bay.

7

Rickshaws to Modern Trains

Alongside Hong Kong's high-rise apartments and office buildings there are reminders of life as it used to be. At the harbor on Hong Kong Island, old-style rickshaws can be hired. The word rickshaw comes from the Japanese *riki* (power) and *sha* (carriage). A rickshaw is a small open carriage on wheels with two long poles at the front. A man picks up the poles and uses his muscle power to pull the carriage.

The Star Ferry crosses the harbor from Kowloon to Hong Kong Island. The buildings in the background are part of the business district called Central.

A man pulls one of the last few rickshaws at the harbor on Hong Kong Island. The taxi in the photo is now much more commonly hired.

Rickshaws were once commonly used as taxis in Hong Kong and also by families and businesses. The idea of rickshaws started in the nineteenth century. The wife of an American Baptist missionary didn't want to ride in a sedan chair carried by coolies, poor Chinese laborers. She wanted to make their job easier, so her husband designed a rickshaw, which is like a sedan chair on wheels.

In the late 1940s there were as many as 8,000 rickshaws on the streets of Hong Kong and it was still an important type of transportation. By the mid-1980s there were fewer than 20 rickshaws left. The Hong Kong government issued the last rickshaw license in 1975 and doesn't intend to issue any more. The rickshaw "boys" who are left are aged 60 and over. They earn money by giving short rides to tourists and by charging to have their photos taken.

Star Ferry

While a short rickshaw ride is now expensive for tourists, the Star Ferry is a real bargain. These large ferry boats regularly cross the harbor between Hong Kong Island and Kowloon. The ride only takes seven minutes and it passes a great mixture of boats. Old-fashioned Chinese junks are still common, and sampans with motors (called *Walla Wallas*) are mostly used to take crews ashore from ships in the harbor. There are also large freighters and tankers. Riding from Kowloon, the ferry heads toward the impressive skyline of Hong Kong Island with its panorama of tall glass and concrete. Other ferry services run to the outer islands.

Trams and minibuses

Ferry services across the harbor started in 1870. About 30 years later the trams that run along Hong Kong Island were introduced. These started in 1904 and now rattle along streets crowded with automobiles and buses.

Colorful trams run across the northern part of Hong Kong Island. These trams were built in the 1950s and 1960s following the design of original trams early this century.

The Peak Tram began in 1888, and it offers a steep ride up to a high area on Hong Kong Island called "The Peak." The tram itself has been running for over 100 years; service stopped during World War II and for an especially violent rainstorm in 1966. Until 1924, when the first road opened, the tram was the only way to get up the hill other than on foot or by sedan chair. The Peak itself is where the wealthy chose to live because it is slightly cooler, and is away from the heavy summer heat in the city. Tourists take the Peak Tram to the top where the view includes Hong Kong Island, as well as Kowloon across the harbor in the distance.

Besides trams and buses there are also minibuses. These are more flexible, stopping wherever people want to get on and off. Minibuses are pale yellow with red stripes down the side, and they seat about 14 people. They can be hailed anywhere, just like taxis. To get off, passengers simply call out to the diver.

Overland and underground

People can also travel below ground on Hong Kong Island and in Kowloon on the Mass Transit Railway (MTR). The MTR opened in 1979. It is fast, cheap, clean, efficient and is the envy of many other cities. Carriages are extra wide to handle very busy rush-hour traffic.

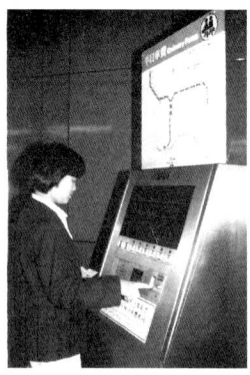

A girl buys a ticket to ride the Mass Transit Railway (MTR). Underground trains run along the routes shown on the map above the machine. The top routes are in Kowloon and a line connects down to a route along the top of Hong Kong Island. Plastic tickets come out of the machine and are put through turnstiles when passengers enter and exit.

The only railroad service in the territory is the line that runs from Kowloon into Canton. The Kowloon-Canton Railway (KCR) runs through the New Territories to the Chinese border and from there passengers change trains and travel into China. The line is now partially electrified. Trains into China are very modern, but have old-fashioned lace curtains on the windows.

Kai Tak airport
The international airport in Kowloon is one of the few world airports still located within a city. It is slightly unnerving as you fly into Hong Kong for the first time. The plane dips and dives and just seems to miss the high-rise buildings as it swoops in to land. The many neon lights of Hong Kong glow constantly and are not allowed to flicker with on-off displays. This is so that pilots will not be distracted by the runway lights as they come in to land. Over 30 world airlines fly to Hong Kong, and it is one of the busiest places in Asia for visitors.

Newspapers, broadcasting, and communications

Hong Kong is also one of the publishing and printing centers of Asia. More than 60 newspapers and about 500 periodicals are produced in Hong Kong. Most are in Chinese but a few English language papers are published as well. There are ten radio channels and four television channels. Some channels broadcast in English, but most use the Chinese language.

Hong Kong uses advanced communications systems. Telephones are very reliable and all local

A man picks up a telephone by a store and makes a free call. There is no charge for local calls so stores often have phones freely available that the public may use.

calls from private phones are free. Only a rental for the phone is charged. Many shops have phones that customers use freely. Telephones are available on the outside of stores, which people simply stop and use.

8 Mahjong to Space Museum

Pastimes in Hong Kong vary from the very old to the very new, from *mahjong* to wind-surfing. Mahjong is a favorite game, which dates from the time of the Chinese Sung Dynasty (960–1279). The original game used 40 pieces of paper, each with a picture on one side. Today brick-shaped tiles less than an inch long are used. They are hand-engraved with Chinese characters and patterns.

Mahjong starts with a roll of the dice. The object of the game is to "go out" by matching tiles of similar values or suits. It is played fast and noisily. There is clacking and banging of tiles as they are slammed down with loud shouts from players. Walking down the streets you hear the clickity-clacking of tiles inside buildings, and the game is played out-of-doors as well. Mahjong is usually played at wedding receptions, before the feast takes place.

Horse racing
Horse racing is nearly Hong Kong's national sport. This is one of the few legal ways to gamble in Hong Kong, and the races attract thousands of people. There are two large tracks, one on Hong Kong Island and another at Sha Tin.

Water sports
Sailing, water-skiing, wind-surfing, and diving are all enjoyed around Hong Kong. Hong Kong is

not known for especially beautiful beaches, but despite this, many are crowded with people escaping the city heat. Beaches are a popular place for young people to meet boyfriends and girlfriends, as happens in many countries. More unique to Hong Kong is an activity called "junking." This is picnicking on the water aboard a large Chinese fishing junk converted into a pleasure craft.

Land sports and rest gardens

Tenpin bowling is one of the favorite year-round indoor sports for all ages. Roller skating, ice skating, tennis, badminton, squash, and golf are popular as well. In the evening, the courts in Victoria Park are floodlit, and basketball is enjoyed by both males and females. Soccer is also played.

In this Kowloon rest garden some men have gathered together to play cards. Chinese cards are very long and thin.

Tai chi is not so much a sport as a traditional kind of Chinese outdoor exercise. The skill in tai chi is to exercise great control when moving slowly from one position to the next. The Chinese gather in parks, moving together through the routine of slow rhythmic exercises.

Hong Kong has rest gardens that are like very small parks where people can do exercises or just sit and talk. Old men gather in small groups, some curled up on benches or the concrete with their shoes off. Playing card games or Chinese checkers (marbles that are moved on a board from hole to hole) is very popular. Some people who do not have a home in overcrowded Hong Kong sleep in the rest gardens on folding beds.

Museums and parks

Hong Kong offers four museums of art, a museum of history, and a wax museum. All the personalities in the wax museum are Chinese, apart from Marco Polo. There is also a Museum of Teaware with 500 pieces of Chinese teaware dating from the seventh century.

An unusual museum is the Sung Dynasty Village in the New Territories, which opened in 1979. This took five years to build, and it recreates life as it was during the Sung Dynasty in China 1,000 years ago, in the years 960–1279. Everything is made as it would have been in the past, and the staff dress in Sung costume. There are craftsmen and shops, recreated old houses, and performances that include a traditional wedding ceremony. This is all as unusual and exciting to a Hong Kong child as it is to tourists.

The Sung Dynasty was a rich time in Chinese

Ocean Park
Hong Kong families often go to Ocean Park, which opened in 1977. This is the world's largest oceanarium. A seven-minute cable car ride takes visitors up to the giant aquarium and Ocean Theater, where there are performances by dolphins, sea lions, and killer whales.
In 1984, Water World was opened with giant slides, a wave pool, and rapid rides. There is also an amusement park featuring one of the world's longest roller coasters.

Sung Dynasty Village buildings in the style used many centuries ago contrast with new apartments in the background.

history and the dynasty also has a close link with Hong Kong. Emperor Ping, the last emperor of the Sung Dynasty, fled south and died in what is now Kowloon.

People visiting the village can buy cookies and candies made from very old Chinese recipes. Visitors can also see a Manor of Nobility, which shows what a rich person's home was like at that time. Craftsmen from China spent years carving the wood, using old methods and tools.

Another unusual park is Tiger Balm Gardens. The founder was a Chinese millionaire who made money with the famous cure-all "Tiger Balm," which is used to relieve asthma, headaches, sore throats, scorpion bites, and other ailments. The garden, built in 1935, is on a steep hillside and has plaster figures showing characters from Chinese folktales and Buddhist stories.

Nightlife

Big city entertainment includes everything from nightclubs and discos to cinemas. American and British films are popular, as are kung-fu films.

Street markets are crowded with food stalls and tables piled with clothing, jewelry, and other goods. Temple Street market is on the Kowloon side and is busy until nearly midnight. The big night market on the Hong Kong Island side is called The Poor Man's Nightclub because wandering through it is a cheap and very entertaining way to spend an evening. As well as vendors selling goods and food, there are story-tellers, minstrels, and even fortune-tellers. One fortune-teller uses trained birds to pick cards that tell a person's fortune.

Neon lights blaze across city streets at night. These lights are at a place in Kowloon called Mong Kok, which is the most densely populated place on earth.

Arts

In Hong Kong there are both Western and traditional Chinese styles of painting. The same is true for performances of music and dance. For example, there is the Hong Kong Philharmonic Orchestra and the Hong Kong Ballet Company as well as Cantonese opera.

Cantonese opera is a very Chinese-style entertainment, with many performances held on

Dancers perform a traditonal Chinese dance, with fans.

the streets and at temple fairs. Performances of Chinese opera are usually held in bamboo mat theaters that are put up temporarily in a public area. During an opera the audience might be walking around, chatting, and even eating. The performances may last from three hours to an entire day.

In an opera, the story is helped along by the way hands, costumes, and faces are moved. There are 50 gestures for hands alone. The main female performer in an opera may wear pheasant tails measuring 5 feet, attached to her headdress. She shows anger by dropping her head and shaking it so that the feathers move in a circle. Surprise may be shown by "nodding" the feathers. The colors of the costumes are important, with yellow the color for emperors and green the color for a person of high rank.

Space Museum

A much more recent addition is the Space Museum on the waterfront at Kowloon. The museum opened in 1980 and has a 300-seat Space Theater where films are projected on the 75 foot domed roof. There is also a Hall of Solar Systems, an exhibition hall, a lecture hall, and an astronomy bookshop. A set of scales gives out a card showing a person's weight as it would be on several planets. Visitors can also choose an area of Hong Kong and can see what it looks like from space. The pictures were taken by Landsat, the first Earth Resources Technology Satellite, launched in 1972. All this is a reminder that Hong Kong is an up-to-date center for world business and trade.

9

Making and Selling Goods to the World

Modern Hong Kong has few raw materials of worth, except for the skills and energy of its people. The territory lives by turning raw materials from elsewhere into finished goods, and by trading and organizing. Hong Kong makes its money by assembling and processing, as well as by shipping, insurance, air freight, commerce, and communications.

Hong Kong first moved into manufacturing in the mid-1950s. It was really a move for survival. In the early 1950s, the United Nations banned many exports to the People's Republic of China. The UN blamed China for "aggression in Korea," and Hong Kong had no choice but to go along with the ban. This meant that Hong Kong lost nearly a third of its foreign trade earnings overnight. Hong Kong began to think about what else it could do to earn its way in the world, and the solution was to turn to manufacturing.

Manufacturing is now the mainstay of Hong Kong and accounts for about 36 percent of all jobs. Most industries are quite small and 90 percent of industries employ fewer than 50 people. There are good geographical reasons why so much industry is light manufacturing. With so much pressure on space, there is not room for large-scale heavy manufacturing. There are no heavy engineering, no big steel plants, no motor industry, and no large-scale shipbuilding. Hong Kong has had to focus on industries needing only

Jeans are sold in a street market. Hong Kong also produces very elegant designer clothes for some of the world's most fashionable stores.

small premises and simple machines. One advantage is that these industries can switch from making one thing to another very quickly. Nearly 70 percent of all workers in industry make cloth (textiles), clothing, electronics, plastics, toys, watches, and clocks, which made up about 80 percent of the territory's exports in the mid-1980s.

In these factories in the industrial area of Kowloon, conditions are often not as good as workers in countries like the United States and Great Britain would expect.

Textiles

The first industry to start up in Hong Kong was textiles. Many of the refugees who came from China in the early 1950s had worked in textile factories, and they brought their skills with them to Hong Kong. In the 1960s, textiles were a very big part of Hong Kong's foreign trade, including nearly 70 percent of exports. By 1973, Hong Kong had become the world's leading exporter of textiles. In the mid-1980s, the textile and clothing industries were still employing about 42 percent of the industrial work force and producing 41 percent of the value of exports.

Why move from textiles?

Hong Kong's success at exporting textiles caused rich Western nations like the United States and Great Britain to worry. Workers in Hong Kong are paid less than in America or the United Kingdom, so products can be made more cheaply. Countries like Great Britain were worried about their own workers. The United Kingdom was the first country to put a limit on textile imports from Hong Kong, in 1954. In 1974 there was a more general worldwide Multi Fiber Arrangement. This further limited the amounts of textiles poorer "developing" places like Hong Kong could send to richer countries. As Hong Kong felt the restrictions, it moved to develop other industries. This was a wise move, since Hong Kong was getting competition from textiles sold by other poorer countries.

The adaptability of Hong Kong's light manufacturing industries and the flexibility of its Chinese labor pool helped it quickly move away from dependence on textiles, and allowed it to take advantage of the boom in the electronics industry.

Other light industries

Electronics is the second-largest export industry for Hong Kong. A wide range of products are made, from calculators, radios, cassette recorders, televisions, and photocopying equipment to microcomputers. In addition, making copies of leading brands and selling them at a cheaper price is big business for Hong Kong. What looks like a name-brand tape or a designer handbag may be just a good copy.

The main product of the plastics industry is toys. Other important light industries make optical and photographic goods, electrical appliances, luggage, and handbags. Hong Kong is now the world's biggest exporter of watches and toys. The textile industry is becoming less important as these other industries grow.

Printing

Printing is another industry that is growing in Hong Kong. There are over 3,000 printing plants and many produce books and catalogs for other countries. Someone going to school in North America, Great Britain, or Australia may find that many of their full-color schoolbooks are printed in Hong Kong. The quality is high, and it is often cheaper for publishers to print in Hong Kong than to print in North America or Europe. One printing house even prints Barbie doll comics.

Hong Kong as a free port

One reason that Hong Kong is growing so fast is that it is a free port. Free ports are areas near seaports or airports where goods are let in without having to pay customs duty. These free ports vary in size but there are now over 400 in 70 countries. The idea has grown since the first one opened in Shannon, Ireland, in 1959.

Beside letting in goods duty-free, these areas offer special deals to industries manufacturing for export. Many electronics, sports goods, and clothing goods are made in such zones by foreign-owned companies. Over 90 percent of what is made in Hong Kong is then exported.

Foreign companies are also attracted by the

Annie Wong of the Tin Fung Printing Press is busy on the telephone arranging work for customers. In the background is an artist pasting-up type and illustrations.

cheaper labor in Hong Kong. Part of the change in world manufacturing is that industries using a lot of labor are moving production to less developed countries where wages are lower.

Hong Kong is now even an investor itself. About 70 percent of overseas investment in China's Shenzhen Special Economic Zone comes

89

from Hong Kong. Manufacturers from Hong Kong, especially in the electronics industries, are moving to Shenzhen to take advantage of cheaper workers and the lower land prices there.

Industrial workers

Workers in Hong Kong industry often work a six-day week, with as few as seven days of paid vacation a year. (They have 17 public holidays as well.) There are no minimum wages as Hong Kong does not belong to the International Labor Organization, which sets working standards. Workers do not get unemployment insurance, either. However, there are laws about the minimum working age.

Trade unions in Hong Kong are not very strong, as Chinese religion teaches that the main loyalty of a worker is to the employer rather than to fellow-workers. Conditions for some industrial workers are not as good as workers in countries such as America or Great Britain would expect.

Bargains for shoppers

Lower production costs in Hong Kong and the fact that goods from elsewhere enter duty-free make Hong Kong a good place for shopping. Gold jewelry is one of the best buys, and Hong Kong is also one of the world's largest diamond-trading centers. Optical goods, watches, electrical products, cameras, film, computers, shoes, and handbags are all good values. Tailors make made-to-order suits and Hong Kong is one of the world's largest exporters of fur garments. Craftsmen make furniture of bamboo, rattan, and cane, and use teak and rosewood as well.

A man makes wire baskets on Ladder Street, Hong Kong Island. The street is really just a long, steep flight of stone steps with a few stalls at the sides. There used to be many more stalls with crafts being made and sold.

Hong Kong is also the world's biggest market for ivory. Shops sell items from toothpicks to chess sets and large carvings. Ivory is a material, like jade, which the Chinese prize highly. (Ivory comes from elephant tusks, and many countries now limit ivory imports to try and protect the world's elephants.)

Hong Kong is a treasure trove for handicrafts, arts, and antiques. There are carpets and rugs from India, Iran, and China. Large department stores such as The China Products Co., Ltd., sell Chinese ceramics, musical instruments, and kites, as well as clothes and herbal medicines.

Stores tend to open late, but they close late as well. They often open seven days a week, although most department stores close on Sundays. Opening hours may be from 10 a.m. to 6 or 7:30 p.m., but many stores, including large department stores, are open from 10 a.m. to 9:30 p.m. Shopping seems to go on even later than these official hours. People can be seen trying on eyeglasses in an optical shop at 10:30 at night. Brightly lit street markets sell goods even later than that, with customers buying shirts, watchbands, or handicrafts at nearly midnight.

Even outside the markets, the streets of a city area like Kowloon are alive and bustling. Street hawkers have carts from which they sell hot food, drinks, and other goods. These carts usually disappear in an instant if the police appear. The government is trying to move street traders into market buildings, but street selling seems part of Hong Kong life. In the city areas of Hong Kong Island and Kowloon, there are 56 markets with over 8,000 stalls selling different goods.

Chinese ceramic pots are just some of the goods sold at the China Products Co., Ltd. stores.

Western district

The area of Hong Kong Island known for its craftsmen is called Western. Western runs along the northwest of the island, and it is the place to see old Hong Kong. In the back alleyways people in small shops and stalls make and sell everything from wire baskets to mahjong tiles. There are fan-makers, carpenters, blacksmiths, and chop-makers who carve name stamps. One street, called Hollywood Road, has shops with both real antiques and reproductions, all of which are bought by bargaining.

In Western you still see much that is traditionally Chinese, and shopkeepers still using an abacus. This is an ancient device for adding and subtracting. Small beads are flicked up and

A mother in jeans carries her baby in a traditionally embroidered cloth strap.

down struts in a rectangular frame to add up the customer's bill. The ancient Chinese instrument for measuring is called a *ching*. This is a pole or stick hanging from a rope with a movable weight dangling from it. In open markets or at the harbor, fish are often sold this way. A woman selling fish, newspapers, or vegetables may well have a baby tied to her back by a traditional, colored cloth strap, often beautifully embroidered. Boutiques in Hong Kong may sell the latest trends in world fashion, but shops also sell *mien lap*. This is the Chinese word for traditional coats stuffed with cotton padding. These are ideal for keeping out the winter chill.

Hong Kong as city-state

The old Chinese ways contrast sharply with the busy financial center. Some people may still use the abacus and the ching, yet Hong Kong also has a gold market that had the third largest turnover in the world in the mid-1980s. Hong Kong has grown rapidly, not least in making goods and selling them to the world. Whatever happens in 1997, what was described in 1841 as a "barren rock" will return to China as a very well-developed, sophisticated and industrious city-state.

Index